Patricia Sykes lives and writes in the Dandenong Ranges, Victoria. She has received New Work grants from the Australia Council and Arts Victoria. Her first collection, *Wire Dancing* (Spinifex Press, 1999) was commended in the Anne Elder and the Mary Gilmore awards for 2000. This is her second collection.

MODEWARRE:
HOME GROUND

Patricia Sykes

Spinifex Press Pty Ltd
504 Queensberry Street
North Melbourne, Vic. 3051
Australia
women@spinifexpress.com.au
http://www.spinifexpress.com.au

First published 2004

Edited by Jennifer Strauss
Cover design by Deb Snibson
Typeset by Claire Warren
Printed and bound by McPherson's Printing Group

National Library of Australia
cataloguing-in-publication data

Sykes, Patricia, 1941– .
  Modewarre : home ground.
  ISBN 1 876756 50 0.
  1. Australian poetry – 21st century. I. Title.
A821.4

This project has been assisted by the Commonwealth Government through the Australia Council, its arts funding and advisory body.

for my sons Terry and Warren

ACKNOWLEDGEMENTS

I would like to thank the editors of the following publications where some of these poems first appeared, sometimes in earlier forms: *The Age*, *Big Bridge* (USA—Online), *Blue Dog*, *Divan* (Online), *Fusebox* (USA—Online), *Island*, *Meanjin*, *papertiger: new world poetry* (CD-ROM), SALT-LICK *New Poetry*, *Southerly*. My thanks also to the relevant organisers and judges for the following awards: 'sanctuary: Swan Lake, Phillip Island' won the Tom Collins Poetry Prize 2002. 'Modewarre — ways you might approach it' was Highly Commended in the Josephine Ulrick Poetry Prize 2002.

I am grateful to the Australia Council, and through it the Australian taxpayer, for the grant which helped make the writing of this collection possible. Particular thanks to Susan Hawthorne and Renate Klein, and all at Spinifex, for their continuing commitment to poetry in a time of increasing challenge to smaller presses. My thanks also to Deb Snibson for the inspired cover design, to Claire Warren for her attentive typesetting, and to Gertrud Kurtz for permission to use her clay sculpture, *Untitled* (1991), as the cover image. Special thanks to Jennifer Strauss for her thoughtful and careful reading of the poems.

The line, 'Do you think for a moment we were human beings to them?', which I've used as the inscription to 'dis-locations . . . a polemic', is from the poem 'The Garden Shukkei-en' in *The Angel of History* by Carolyn Forché (1994, Harper Collins).

CONTENTS

HOUSE OF WATER

HOUSE OF DETENTION

HOUSE OF THE BIRD

Modewarre — ways you might approach it

1 difficulties with maps

because the syllables
on the page are not
the land beneath the name

because a childhood memory
of place is not the same lake
upon which the duck floats

because a grandmother
got Modewarre factually wrong
as '*that backwater*

where snakes come backwards
out of their holes'
and because of the woman

with the head of a bird
who placed her ancient skull
in a cold stare against my own

the implacable kiss—
a silence inhuman
in its lack

her visible intent
to be a disturbance
in the blood

as a pulse which meanders
among the maps
which do not exist

2   acts of identity

because this is a place of death
it is necessary to resort to books
skin of the plant on which ink

mimics the intrinsic knowledge
of worms   who being earthed
have their heads deep into it

doubly advantaged by there-ness
and an un-need for meanings
it's the humming plastics though

of telephone speech not of worm
or page which confirms '*yeah . . .
modewarre . . . it's Wathaurong*

means musk duck'   (place of?)
laconic breeze of the vernacular
laid over enforced extinction

of a language   the whole country
dotted with such deaths
but in the phone voice the absence

of revenge mocks any expectation
of it   by the Wathaurong co-op
I'm helped to understand

that research is on the road
to raise the culture up
I'm helped on to Bruce Pascoe

who helps me on to the posthumous
Lou Lane her boxed white pages
in the Geelong Records Office

un-indexed are fraught
with European-in-origin
local-by-birth   offspring

of the irony of method
working for years to retrieve
what cannot be given back

all breath here is spent or spending—
bird you flee from the archives
like a patient escaping the knife

and now again the road is a bare desk
and you a dark-feather creature
since the time before biblical

like wings against distance
growing now more lucid
now less clear   unto yourself

and a speck also   burning
and watering in the eye like a splinter
out of this a lake rises and rises

it may yet prove an inland sea
the wraith of it says *yes let the eyes weep*
let them   they have need of consequences

3   ancestral

three roads meeting in the one bird:

> *modewarre* (the indigenous)
> *biziura lobata* (the colonial)
> *musk duck* (the common)

between them everything ancestral
their one lung the breath
below water and above it

'and so I am of the junction
and so my tongue rises to be born'
had she lived to draw breath

my mother's last stillborn
may well have said this—
but would she have meant born

to communal or to corporate?
in the epochs of takeover
the umbilical is as necessary

as lifeline
the duck delivers and delivers
the shining eye of water

the play and gleam of it
as it rolls lightly off the feathers
back into its own cup

if it were as possible to live
in the recombined moment
but we accrue as the roads accrue

and the accretions become
at their worst a flotilla
siblings of the first fleet

the wretched journey
that came ashore as a haunting
—as always the modewarre

places faith in its eggs
yolk and the sun
breed each other

in the house of the bird
the embryo in its shell turns
to the arms of its oxygen

4   generation

the return that began in dirt
the wet and dry embrace of it
its reach into every orifice

its hold on the throat
bird you have drawn me
to the brown lake   end

of the easy picnic   a food haze
dying in its own romantic
and you emerging as the brackish

tang of a bird in water
that swims so low it seems
to drown   an in-hiding

a v-wake of dark ribbons
their glossy drag of secrets
like a tug in the pulse

it's not your Kulin life I'm after
its recovering geographies
but how to go on

from here   my feet
live off bones   my words
play across old veins

what I eat I devour
what I touch fingers me
with scars   it's the same

new song   progress loves
the individual   the ethic
of rewarded self   poetry

cannot speak for the whole
it is too full of variants
how then to evolve back to water?

5   the bird as it is found

at midday   deep in its brown lake
–the sun warming the same compass–
the chevrons and rivulets of the bird's

rippling wake a water entranced
and the oxygen separating itself out
in small flashing leaps

at play as an ecstasy of bubbles
here is proof of the bird books:
the heavy body   the low swimming

habit   the legs set well back
for the diving life   the male darker
grey than the female's brownish

charcoal   he in solitary water
displaying himself   the inflated
throat pouch the honk the whistle

the churning splash   a breaking of light
into shimmer crystals but the people
are charmed by the swans

and the female musk duck is busy
feeding her single young
odd that the books forgot

to note the delicate accuracy
with which she passes
lake shrimp to her duckling's

equally dexterous bill
the swans on irritated
surface patrol forcing her

to combine evasion with the hunt
she is good at this
her predatory skills

keeping swans and duckling
likewise on edge
until abruptly hunt becomes preen

one moment the dive
then the drift to safe water
a haven among water lilies

pink and waxy with succulence
dense raft of protective greens
this is luxury time

this magnet to danger
as the soft paler belly rolls
upwards in preening exposure

how quickly the young must learn
the way of it   the swift massage
and flick back to hide the beautiful target

the snatched rest a midday snack
the lake dredge with its steel teeth
already back in the poisoned

muds   the road traffic
as the rise and fall
of familiarity's warning revs

how ironically pure at this moment
that the current should roughen
and the clouds come driving in with rain

—chill of the returning hours
the ducks refreshed in their feathers
disturbed into moving on

in such safety as is theirs
their waters still historical
still urgent to be read

11

song of walking

having come so far, having gone—
this way and none other
the ever hidden duck
who had planned to be a silence
it is known her voice added weight
to *creator* and *beginning*
that where she touched air water land
whoever follows has to make a choice
'*the fish will fight you*
for their lives
the geese claim their own wings
against the winter
the frogs have a reason
to suspect poisons…'
                      breathe! breathe!
is this why the duck teaches caution?
how once she gave permission
for a landing and was invaded
by desperates sprouting sails
from their backs?   now
an historian writes of strangers who
dance to each other upon the shore
as if they have the sheen upon them
so that when they spread their footprints
they can become not plague but proposition
clearly something hears a music—
what more is there to say of longing?

toxic, kiss

i

whether it was done boldly or with stealth
whether the faces were strange or known

official or private, when they came
among the food, in the day, the night

to conduct their little murders

> *'modewarre, how far were you*
> *from the poisoned flour*
> *the water laced with arsenic?'*

ii

verse, chorus, anthem, voice
the history wars of mixed blood

and split opinion
the duck keeping no records

except for memory,
here, this place

iii

> —once, our house Modewarre's small timbers
> singing in the night and the stars howling
> because the child heard them

from deep inside the kiss of deadly nightshade
purple berries and delicious orgy
smeared across the lips of her pale infancy

we do not call her innocent
we call her blessed, survived,
and talk of what can kill

iv

—after all it is safer in the kitchen not to stagger
food wants always to be trusted but is always in the hands

the duck itself wishes to feed no surgery no medi care
sister, your belladonna is Italian somewhere else, where

Mussolini lived   was fascism ever here?
the duck knows   and the eras   '*don't grieve them*'

—only begin again   where it began as the confidence
of water   everything touchable, and closer

duck psalms

1st psalm

not to deify you, duck, as a god life
a servant of history   enthroned
tyrannical   impossibly endowed

and you so dark-grey and immiscible
only once have I seen your true feet
they were webbed and animal skinned

and sure of their water, its weeds, its
muds, the life that feeds and is fed upon
—bird without need of a reliquary

there's talk of clever nets and night traps
photography too is on the snatch   praise
rather to your bird way of tenable and proof

2nd psalm

the slanting rain-veils across the paddocks
were never a sign of your coming or going
you never there beside the child on her knees

who nightly on brown lino was taught feathers
are skies of angels, heavenly more feasible
than any duck's power to call down miracles

but she was obstinate that girl and left her ghost
behind, a hankering for real wings, the flight
you use only rarely it seems, as if having this

is reason neither for jubilation nor proof, but bird
when you preen there is a touch of something
like faith, a pleasure even, that this is so

3rd psalm

and of course you were there, like a secret
behind the second eyelid; praise to whoever
sees without having to be forced; praise to

whoever looks beyond the lure bird;
when we came with our firesticks and farming
it was poverty's golden goose we were chasing

our hunting skills threadbare and makeshift
and though we never ate you bird we ate your
relatives and never called ourselves cannibal

4th psalm

and now language, so impossibly cumbersome
for discovering the true weight of things
the grandmother would have known

the heft of you, duck, the right size dish
for the oven; you'd have been her novena
of gratitude, a meal stolen from the mouth

of starvation   if you were in her grasp
would I have played ingratitude's child?
I think your eyes, those black carbons

would have gone the way of mutton
'food is food' she'd have said,
'myth is myth'

5th psalm

our kindling in its fire-making
lighting neither flame nor image of you
the kitchen's red music oblivious

to the wind's chimney song of a bird
we never learned but the pianola days
could have trapped you, duck

inside the nostalgia of pop song
I'll be your angel you be my wings—
all power then to the bird that went

about its own lyrics, all honour to
the same bird whose daily water
is its necessary choir

6th psalm

the hymns that lived in our small rooms
how they flew from our mouths as
inflations of hope, the art of vanishing

to live among fly specks on the ceiling
lead paint also lived there
and the greasy smoke of rations

the war dead and their anniversaries
over and over the same yearly candles
but there were incubations, duck

and though we sank our necessary well
it was not to drain your wetlands
it was that sweet water meant baptism

each bucketful an evidence of home
each new infant's deeper chance of roots
each stillbirth another travel lesson

7th psalm

when we left in our sad ambulance
you were still invisibly watered some-
where between kero lamp and starlight

the unmade roads had no compass
leading to nest or feeding ground
our only car pointed towards town

how we were engined and rubber tyred
there was no-one to make a grief over you
a corner shop was our new adoration

I think you did not bother to sing praise
at our going, though it has taken years
to plot this return to sing *you*, therefore

blessed is the duck whose indifference
is survival, blessed also is the duck for whom
worship is a human thing, strange, even pitiable

conjuring under the influence

the festivals have left for us their careful litter
all the smoked days between have not killed
fresco and proof, bird and domain, gold sheaf
and solar warning   the mirror wetlands
always find us   think of the goddess in
her ritual room wearing her necklace of ducks
in the prayer it will ensure both people and bird
as if *'futile'* never hurt her   her knowing
that mutual fertility is no defence   the rain
pouring off the window is her own lost river
the glinting silver speed of it, the cold roar
I wade the room hunting each piece of broken bird
there's a neck here stretched like a duck's in flight
naked and shining   the way feathers gleam their
oily way through the wet   the wattage droops
the temperature shivers, which makes perfect
voltage sense, and still the neck aims itself
towards the sun, hope and yellow fed, wholly
adorned by the embroiled heart's freight

eupathy

under the ribcage
the magma at red heat
we meet
between the furnace and the flying

in the mouth of cohabitation
beneath that other river
the air
dark arc of soaring

when eagles are there
stream of current and
thermal beckoning, riddled
with holes

in open season
or when eagles as supects
were killed by lambs
these farmed in law

as a greater claim
so that it was air
that hovered
looking down upon

the hung Bunjils*
their stopped feathers
strung wing-tip to wing-tip
upon the barbed fences

to talk now
of whether this is still so
or if the eagles in free flight
are an option

to speak of
options, land, again
once more
not as that which was taken

is un-ownable
contracting and crowded
but as lava shift
the heat of a river

always underfoot
in a molten indifference
to politics, how the height
of an eagle

---

* eagle creator being of the Wathaurong

knows this
its kill days
numbered to our care
while brain years plan an escape

to the stars   what difference
could we commit there
that would make human
safer

less
of a threat?
do the restless feet
know

does the orbiting mind?
or is this just a voice
from the dark matter
of fear

afraid of reach
and plot-based ambition?
as if should the eagles fall
so will the piercing eye

'brid',* eight darknesses

i

no belling
by the identity tag
no raucous telling of a
knowledge's secret necessity
the brid's closed throat
somewhere warmer
held, than this gallery
this arrested buying

ii

to desire flight but be human
to own legs but come home
with wings, a falling into
a sky I must believe in
no hum to it, no ticking
only this sung silence
awake and dreaming

---

* The name given by Nyangangu to her bird carving.
Nyangangu is a Yolgnu artist of Northeast Arnhem Land.

iii

the wings infolded
in a dark body
the weight in the body
like floating
hush-la, hush-la
no lullaby but the blood
the brid who never sleeps
its heart's alacrity
which is machete born

iv

—Nyangangu, you carve
like peeling back the skin
inside the brid the next live
brid, there, where you are,
bred of earth, breeding sky
working the uplift, wingbeat
as if sculpting a refusal
to die of white history

v

to take broken eggs
and give them flight
to take invasion
and find the sky in it
how difficult
how simple
to place a machete
inside the tongue
and sing morning and night
to keep survival tuned

vi

daughter of the daughter
of a warrior, the brid
each day leaving my room
each day returning, amid
whether the money I paid
is a cage
though air visits us freely
and daily I warn myself—

vii

it may be financial need
your living to earn
but, Nyangangu
I think you must own
great faith
to trust your brids
to any random house

viii

or not just need but a reaching?
the brid's upstretched throat
forever in natal song
north of this keyboard's
tireless tap-tap mouth
which cannot voice
the interior 'n' in Nyangangu
the one with the tail
the sound of 'ng' in singer

espionage with duck

if it looks like a duck and talks like a duck
it must be a government surveillance device

this not in the wisdom texts
but in the weird science
of an artificial eye whose wine
is calamity in the cellar—
I find you in the museum Wiesbaden
is really code for *a duck's quack*
has no echo, which is silenced
easily therefore, the shimmer
of plumage and gland of musk
fallen to the gaze, or else to the palate
where transformation is skill of the chef
where the bird who once flew becomes
meat with hot and cold properties,
is a pianist playing, the main course,
with oranges and wild mushrooms
and contextual candles melting
under the heat of Rachmaninoff
but I think for the woman
with cutlery still alive in her hands
the electronic eye makes a worse salad
its vigilance not half as delicate
as the wings on her plate

blandishments and enticements, visuals of electronic speech

a pixel e-bird myriad and reciprocal   the
idea of a poem as multiple rooms slow-
dragging itself out of the virals   it sits
on a granite slab by the old orchard and
watches the fruit   figs (big, luscious)
oranges, feijoas, grapefruit, kumquats,
their aromatics more or less in favour
of *choose, pick, savour*   and recalls
how dangled food supposedly keeps appetite
up to its motivation

                              between fluidity
and fixity the pilgrim poem begins to turn
cerulean blue   it is thinking of *island*
as metaphor for *self* and wishes to fly there
later, an artist friend e-writes me her theory
that brain cells re-wire themselves when
new images emerge

                    some live some die
we decide our techno-umbilical conversations
are a thin layer of water clarifying our mutual
obsession with elements mirroring each other
as in shredded emotions and the luminous
Mungo sands   it's not the sands that make
us feel phoney   it's the gawk factor, tourism
in the season of 'going there'   our paltry tents

among the dust storms   and thirst so driven
a kangaroo stealths in to drink the dishwater

       what the moon sees the moon exposes
among the now eyes the bones the hard facts sifting
sifting   old fingers of hunger which cannot settle
and why should they why should they if it is only
to make a future comfortable
       'the grief that can be trusted is the one
       that does not defuse itself in optimism'—

remember the flocked galahs at the Walls of China
the wrought change as they stilled their garrulous
pinks and greys to silence and faced the setting sun
the sun dyeing the clouds the same tonal flush
the galahs taking their own colour back into their
feathers   miracle of re-absorption not even
the night's consuming indigo can rob them of—
continuity without loss?   the final room refuses
to close itself   as when in dreams some events
can only be viewed through feathered doors

eponymous

to the interrogator who keeps asking
'so are you still suckling on myths of place?'

I say try the enigma address
the bird who keeps vanishing in water—

if sunrise is the warm traverse across a
cold face, the glacier, say, in a bird's eye

then *thaw* must be the language of *found*?
whatever whole or broken thing, this worst

that best, this life, to call it fiend, roof, faith
to hold its feathers in your hands, to alarm

soothe, confuse, to rephrase the first word
the last, to cut, paste, discard, worse

to let the boots in, to risk the beak, all the
shatter things   *stupid!* how six letters

cannot explain why a thing is done
the bird itself never before so lucid

wanting it undone, wanting the hand
gone, without its mauling the radiance

flamingo, flamenco

after all it was a dream the island of flamingoes
and we are heavier boned not the long leg long
neck elegance of the gracile gone miocene bird
phoenicopterus novae hollandiae
fossil tibiotarsi in the lake

how hungry extinction is for marrow
feathers are never ready to expire
in the dream so many flamingoes
they are sun eternal rise sun eternal set
so many the sky steamily crimson rises
and rises   haven of the fled briny waters
reek of the salts in the birds' upside down beaks
seek and filter   filter and survive

how does it matter
that the birds were at the gone lakes before us?
look that leg that thinks it is a young tree dancing
and that tranced neck gliding through the pink wind
they could have been a violence   a war   turmoil
of the heart's valley   what saves us does not save us
the ghost birds flying up out of the ground the slender
forgotten ones we don't talk about   as if they are
only a memory twinge passing through rosy light

and besides (besides!) on the other continents there
are multitudes   greater lesser   red leg yellow leg
flush of the flocks in their breeding thousands   but
here in one bird   —   a limp body's enfolded wings
asleep in the dream's lap   —   lies a wish for the end
of paralysis   on the rim of a bird bath my dead
grandmother dances again her lifetime candles
at the edge of a bay my bare feet intercept the final
undulations of a scarlet fan shell   hand clap and
castanet   foot stomp and forage and the sea lethal

and prodigious   are you hunting cause?   inside
a climate oscillatory and unpredictable?   inside
the fingerprint of the human aorta? the redball sun
is an eye trying to pierce through pollution clouds
we give money to the brain and let it connive
and always the belief in lyric and experiment

to dream a bird is to decide its future   how not
to fritter its fire   how not to confine it to zoo
or amulet   in southern Spain you can sit
with intimate friends and watch firebirds dancing   -
by moonlight   in the arid centre the red is in the
soil   is in the rock   everywhere the remains
the bird has already given itself   the flame still
on its feet   unafraid of itself   unafraid of us

House of Water

three years in the flooded paddock

1   tussock as sign language

the tussocks so at home
they pass through the wind
as if rustle and click
is the language of clarity
no word for such voices
but they're reading you
in their plant-like way
siphoning the feel
of you, the taste,
the way they'd siphon air
or ground water
for what's digestible
for what's trouble

       what never was field
       become paddock become
       fences become livestock
       the cattle the sheep
       foraging for the hoofprints
       they lost the last time
       they departed a shore
       'this is the way the feet jump'
       are a child's bare legs
       leaping over the reedy spears

in that awkward straddle
that knows itself shifted
between *home* and *home*—
not every deck as convict
one tussock capsizing her
onto hands and knees
where like a grounded thing
she is learning mud
as delicious and terminal

2   the burgeoning

the night terrors have nothing to defend
the butterfly was due to be woken
susurrus, hiatus, susurrus, pulse rush
and pause   muffled thunk of
the milk urns against her father's thighs
her barometer man as danger's deep
bruise, all the fear day building
to meet his return, since, metal
and flesh, he might grind the hurt
between his teeth and bring it home

until then the day will delope and delope
her sister's small faeces will hit the ground
as warm plosives each one benign and
satisfied, she herself will untie the milk
and loose the calf's frolic and frisk

and she will thank each happy average
against blood positive crossed with blood
negative, the Rh, the monkey, the born,
and the next foetus already on the road
after which there'll be no more haema-
globin, for which she has no word
other than *goblin*, the turkey
upon her tongue, its mad warning
pulling the wind into spurts
from her throat, *gobb-lin, gobb-lin*
though she as third person thinking
she is safe yet, the waters not having
broken and the womb like a country
prepared but here's the truck roaring
and she is wrong she is wrong

3   girl at play on the occasion of her mother's death

the air a cold south and the day not lovely
her father's knife in the yesterday sheep's throat
as the same dread now rushing her pulse, the safe
lamb taken out of her hands, taken out of the cloth
she'll remember the grey chill clouds prolonging
the numb hour, a wallpaper thick and suffocate,
a clag in the lungs, she'll remember every dumb
sodden thing, the bereft horizon provoking
her with its shroud, the ticking omnivorous
minutes, her mother's dress in their wet mouths

here's her own rage (*welcome! welcome!*)
electric with new tenure—
are these her dancing feet?
they are grief's own pistons
they cannot be consoled
and so they rise and fall
and so they crush and crush the day's-eyes
and so a yellow stench anoints the air
and so the death bird is lured
and so she takes aim in its breast
and so the sky blemishes with red
and so scavengers gather to the largesse
and so she spends her breath
among the feathers and the bones
and so at last it is over it is done
and so forever the knife a shining elegy

an answer to crockery

all the faithful years the well
giving from its deep hole

and that mouth your cup
talking and talking of emptiness

as if you are still the small daughter
furthest from the source, laid down

among inner walls of old hessian
their cockroach scuttlings and sinister

rat, where moon or no moon
your safety was the dreams that rocked

that rocked—the warden of urine so asleep
on your sheets you awoke eloquently

as warm reek   the bedwet as clearest
author   therefore don't be subtle

admit the fluids of the page are hers
and require nothing that will dilute her

look, she carries no flask and drinks
only from the rain

to resurface aqua vitae
as water's answer to an empty cup

since like a stricken anniversary
you dry up each winter

for she knows about cold, how it is
easier then to die without vitality

doll archive

the doll was always a sleeper
annually the beautiful swimming
of ducks must have skimmed her
and touched nothing but water
now some hook-toed thing
finding the pockmarks in her,
ripples, a widening, to a colony
of infection, its white useage
of the Wathaurong women
the putting them aside after
as if dolls
     'when glass eyes are oracles
     all you need is deep looking'
the doll might have written this herself
if she bowed to the fluency of lenses
instead she's teaching how to bathe an
infant   soft nape in the novice hands
their steady tremble   say it's how
history unmasks us, these attempts
to hold gently a vulnerable fact:
     is there a hospital for this?

the rasping of crows turning the sky
dark and clever   contagion is
sometimes exquisite—consider the gone
women as a spectral wit   raucous in

humour against the living whose inheri-
tance is the diseased or healthy body of us
all   doll my philosophical, extenuating
no escape   an hour is only an estimate
the danger's in living without a tax on sleep
that breath on the pillow   old lung whose
irruptions make a hole in distant weather

proximities

(i)   the eyes having returned
     are busy as inlets

(ii) the geography not as it was
     but the loony girl still here
     still terribly lustrous

(iii) the lava rocks, how rock on rock
     they are, deep seed and flying dust

       —there were other beginnings, tempting, now lost

       but take the synchronous eyes   as if by naming
       themselves *tidal* they can claim to be interpreters

       and the loony girl, as if she's a luminous mooning
       an Andromeda, though neither sentenced nor chained

       except by a schoolyard pack who craved a target, limpid,
       mother-sheltered, palely sensible in her big-brim hat

       look how she spits into the wind, refusing to play *lost*
       child   found, redemptive—it's true she grew among

       hagiographies   the rocks too are real   impossible
       to play favourites, the small grey one which was a slate

smudge of chalk, smear of jam, drool of plum
or the huge indigo whose breath ached of frostbite

'*fragments do not stand alone*'   strange transport
to be pinned here among cold keys, their provender doors

of increasing rust, the plains laying wreaths at our feet
our pairs of acre children, of the Crown years, advance

and advent, *cops and robbers, what's the time Mr Wolf?*
and for the modewarre, years of treading water

Lake Modewarre cryptids

carnal water and the longing for immersion
all day the bunyips' wash and catastrophe
disturbances in the crust, the core, lap lap
at the shore, a swamp harrier hovers,
around the rim the volcano relics
old misshapens, old toxics, the wind
not now a thing of sulphur, instead this
creature named *most grotesque* of the
feathered, an isolate, impossible to reach
in a day's baffled swim, inside her black
mirrory eye the calm lake floating
which is not food nor refuge nor God—
she can smell you fresh from the pages
too many hours of massacre research
too many footprints leading too far in
the wind pulls tears from the sockets
as if you came for a cleansing, be hard
hard she says not soft's eternal sinking

the honey lands

between night's blackout
and mesmeric kilometres
the car consuming and dwarfed
in the way a journey imagines
itself immortal

infinitude and restlessness
the always direct wind
going straight for the orifices
the thrive the rot the warm devouring

—when did the road get to be so clever
at smelling out the giveaway itineraries
as easily as the tracking of salivas?

*

by the roadside an honesty stall
offering peacock feathers and quinces

at the edge where all wheels gouge
the crumbling of sustenance

as if whimsy has worked endearingly
to outsell the staples

*

thrum! thrum! thrum!
the corrugations of the home road
dust's memoirs on the windscreen
remember this? this? this?
sky and ground remembering roof
and floor, the house of sex
keeping a woman pregnant
as if passion were a weapon
annual and fatal, alive
in this engine whose now oil
the essential is purse of war
bulge, the agony of an ectopic
as from its rifting seams, red,
slowly, blood's viscous leak

*

slipshift the gloriosa shimmer of
sunlight upon rainsoaked leaves
into bone music from under the
trance tyres, percussion of vertebrae,
skulls, the terra nullius dead, until
what will it take to answer them
not with an ANZAC, day of
nation my hero, but jawbone
to cheek   *'in the pain of proximity*
                all excuses are a leaf litter'
as falling day, breaking night
the cave of years keening in our feet
where nothing dies that is committed
unless deliberate   unless buried

aphorisms bluestone and spectral

autumn   to be at the gate, wind on the turn
skin of change, yellow, red, final brown
placing your one life in its circumference

why then fight the old cracked path?
and the door, the chill mornings
to stand here holding them apart

is to garner two cold hands   gather
firewood if you must, the chimney's
smoke signals will not summon what is lost

winter   as now the brittle air lays down its frost
your white breath fraying among the
classroom dead: the *Henries Edwards*

Georges as inscribed in the desks, their
royal pantheons, their chanted dominions
—wasn't it you who said rote learning turns

students into drones?   beware you said
the singsong that kills off native foods by
wielding against them the livestock of kings

summer   when nothing is more inclusive than a bushfire
           enjoy the equality of fear
           this is how architecture learns to be redundant

           the schoolhouse now more nearly toy size
           brought down out of the bluestone solidities
           that on Saturdays hit sixes to God   to come

           this way the fire must have an end in view
           in the flushing out of quarry it is merciless
           it's in its nature to send us fleeing for our lives

spring   Buckley was mostly wrong about the bunyip
           perhaps it was the luscious thaw, the pour of
           fresh water into the lake that made him mistake

           as oversize, calf size, a male musk duck full in
           mating uproar   to feast the eyes on a beast
           half admired half imagined is to paint a myth

           larger than its source; I think he thought he saw
           a regal monstrous thing, let's leave it there
           let no monarchs come hideous and flaunting

sanctuary: Swan Lake, Phillip Island

for there is water and there is sky
and between them feet big with tongues

i

each act of language a collision, each one
a shoe   this one a walking default
in the tracks of a committee

who left signs: 'can you believe
this was once a paddock used for cattle?'
and   'Once a Paddock, now

a Sanctuary'   which makes of the visitor
a kind of tourist-refugee at a ballet
where the dancing swans are black not white

but what I came for is seasonal   a lesson
from the musk duck and indeed I find three
all female   therefore no mating

only the close feathered swimming
that means companionable   a time to eat
between the broods   the noisiest demand

the soft dopple each of them makes
in their feeding dives   a way to cut
water open without forcing a wound

ii

how the eyes like linguists are never satsified
how they'll poke and pry into any lexicon
the ducks unaware they are being watched
(the hides silent as isolation cells)
or so used to reflection   as in
the water-pictures mirrored in binocular glass
that they've adopted their own dictionary
of indifference   they float like calm boats
entice the eyes nearer towards ignorance
until it's impossible to tell if the small
birds skittering beyond them
on the camouflage line between water and sky
are sandpipers or plovers   a failure of image
as language   magnified by distance
identity then as a secret habitat
the lake concedes at least this much
what it offers is light   the slow
fingering drift against the skin
and I think this is how trespass
might be tamed   by vibrations
so intense it agrees to the muzzle

iii

the day so warm it sheds layers
a throat could be thirsty with syllables
and be unable to offer a word

if it has not learned to live
by native food what could it speak
that would keep anything else alive?

on the hide's darkest wall
a namesake has painted a species guide
among the solitary gloom it is like meeting

a faith in the traffic then the failure of it
each time the satellites chatter overhead
the musk ducks avail themselves

of the dive   forgive them
they confuse speech with death
and human with predator-as-alphabet

the efficacy of a lantern on the forehead

'*what do you see when you look at landscape?*'
smoke rolling in like funeral fog
the digital spasms of a water metre
loose ends, loose, fire and drought
and a longing for wet calm, but this
room, that room, the shift, the view
the next one a Franco, elsewhere dead
but here enframed
                    halo, holy, photograph
in this house the tended walls tended
by a woman losing her finger-prints
her hand palely on his shoulder
like a vagina defecting from itself
how can genealogy be so terrifying?
we scar each other like dart lightning
when she says they're related she means
he's paid for, deeds of the house, the taxes,
she spoke once of a Spain where the
Franco-killed went down on their knees
here, there, the republic of blood
yielding less than their names
but on the last visit there are prayers
in the food, and red candles   among
their bright flames *her hunger his silence*
the table's early muscatels in a sugar need
all the warm vines knowing when a wind

is dangerous   *his hunger her silence*
as in replete   as in shrine accomplished
as if   '*ah aromatic aureole   kitchen*
of the intellect   pantry of the appetite'

dura mater

1 pre-med

in the hour before surgery the stones louder
more musical
                  'sibling, sibling'

feet have seen the woman
who carries live pebbles under her tongue

feeding the river   and days and nights
have found their own eyes floating among

them   pinpoint stars   astonished
to be counted among the debris

2 grace notes and your harvest heart

the foetal life reaped and reaping
the sedated womb inept

at keeping out the instruments
whose ancestor is stone:

life loves you, science is
rational, wear the God head

all the soft and hard arguments
living outside the placenta

but having come from there
cut, shoved, or eased out

each with its mouth
open and irrevocable:

'we all cry like babies if we make the world'

as if word has come
of a perfect humanity, how it pours

through the red stab in the abdomen
compassionate as money

3   shatter the breath to come near her

no oasis but the throwers of stone
on behalf of a dogma

as if it is necessary
to break the woman

before the dogma itself is broken
therefore how she shudders

before the hands, the kin
of them, their great passion

as it crushes her bone by vein
to pave the road with—

her face under their feet
and the passing trucks

heavy with quarried rock
as if they are carrying

her last voice —afterbirth
you must be believed

the holy street has drunk her blood
and you bear down into silence

4   sepulture

among the legends that she came
through the Modewarre marshes to breed
and die six feet down between Agnes
and Adelaide and be called anonymous

and gone, her final stillbirth nameless also
among the ruby brilliance of seminar blood
as if all sentiment is frieze, is sepulchre,
test tubes of the river, litter and pour,

the stumble stones bearing teeth marks
tender, bitter, bruise the fleshed epitaph
warm stone echo breath, here, where,
the generations wetting their feet

profit and loss

the house unrequited
in the way squalls

drive in from the ocean
against hot house glass

the windows cannot defray
their white rush

a trawl of waves
gnashing and greeting

among the highs and lows
of post-christmas stocks

whose charts ride and slip
with the urge to drag skin

over yield curves of satin
or put feet

to a breakfast floor
that's not alive with shards

look at this hand
bearing its steel kettle

all the way to the stove—
it cannot ignore

the recurrent leftovers—
like grass brittles in summer

its lips clam and bleed
investing against thin salivas of loss

a face in water

you who left the city with your broken body
to sculpt what might even further come out of you alive

transportation   as when in a time of loss you went missing
and found yourself river-tranced

a face drying in your hands
and breathing began again as fluid wish and

introspect, into your body's red depths
against the injuries, the abattoir

settlement   the drowsy thrill of being woken at sunrise
by a flute's refusal to stalk anything

moving to its own heartbeat
the swoop and catch hours seeming

to trickle here, slow water, navigating
by the senses, safe almost, cocooned

from the hyper life's furious haranguing
only the need to *touch, watch*

the ground, the life, neither for temples
but for templates   and I've seen

what oozed from you, what sprang
what might have lain here

longer, colder, food not from
the vine but of the alluvial tongue

clay   the face in its deep hole bleeding water
through your eye-pits your open mouth

your hands in her, excavated and excavating
is this how you can begin to walk again

limping and reconciled
not mud but the idea of mud

plastic and amenable   given
back to you, in the summer of the river

HOUSE OF DETENTION

blue heimat

so the migrated self painting itself
as fish-netted head, half-torso
with arms left behind, elsewhere
through the blue window, gone
to whatever socket they were torn
from   the left ear facing *now*
the right eye yoked to *then*
trapped in the sepia room's dust
yesterday, today, tomorrow
three cells, three prisoners
loyal as fingerprints
the vast mind's iron bars
and its sightlines in the breastbone
all ache, cure, breath, sky, the sailed
home's blue bribery, blue nostalgia

yes, I can see this, but your blue cow
who wants to be at home in every world
where exile does not exist, nor jargon of
a milk mass produced, only a particular
udder and its particular cream, here,
now, in the cranked up days of terror
where there is no safety in 'either or'
only the blue cow's teats in your blue-vein
hands and how delicately you must take
small enough to keep you both alive

fabulously there is no error, she wears
no bell, but how inhuman she is
the way she can gather her blue breath
and walk off not ever looking back

hard garbage

spaces cry room cry house
cry *try me* as if a small
availability can expand into
what cannot be afforded
or is absent   the found
chance — why should it be
concrete?   you'd think skin
didn't erupt to its own
pleasures   and this
earthquake passing under
on the scale of unrest
what would you be riding
but invisibilities of force
as would crush earth's
furniture and yoke

a ferret in migrant trousers

'inventory legs in a typhoid year, the delirium of change
infecting the fear zones where most rats invade the head
the Nissen huts at Benalla-Benalta place of water place
of exposure coming alive for post WW2's hope ships
& allocation & bedding & cutlery & the sun beating
down upon the assisted migrants' new climatic heads
& they stunned by suffocation's tin army huts, though
no sign of jeeps & soldiers & ammo just handy digs
outside town so the town could sleep safe in its beds
& in time permit mixed weddings to assimilate the
local rag & smiles all round then in the churches
because their congregations swelled like pregnancy
though religion wasn't the same ferret as the one
in the hut of Helmut who loved real ferrets not Hitler
or God & daily he'd shine his buck teeth into his ferret's
heart and once when I'd come to look he took the ferret
from its cage and put its alive animal self down his trousers
& my eyes more warned than sexed up because Helmut
was no scared rabbit no matter what the town wanted'

Hepzibah

of a childhood as musical
as birds singing in the arteries
so the documentary

posthumously   not refraining
but as refrain   her own
and Yehudi's laughter in a spill

                    of secrets
as in the naming themselves
'those incestuous sonata players'

                    the taking
of sister, brother as musician
not lover, but near
to this, acknowledged risk

                    out of the fullness
the forte, the pianissimo, her passion
in leaving

                    the concert halls
for a career of love, the heave
and fluency in her fingers

                    from sonata
to geo shift
from delight to illusion crash
not as if one morning the sun

rose differently
and bled into her, golden
and earnest, or as if a wound

from the plum gardens
made her want
to change self, world

remind us, Hepzibah
how you were always
a thinker, how it was the stifle
by obdurate privileges

a fatal
inability to conform, some call it
restlessness, of spirit

unquenchable
passion, a provocative politics
leading to the stalled

marriage, the children
you left behind more troubling
to yourself, to everyone—

'transgression and the mortal coil'

—how could you have guessed
my *Snow White Laundry* grandmother
in despite of, would extol you

           though not as more
fulfilled than her own hands
strong and steeped, scrubbing
energy back into your sheets

           now that it is years late
to tell you, and of how those you sent her
straight from the stressed body heat
of Jewish evacuees

slowly gave up their horror nights
growing unafraid of exposure
drying openly in the wind

                —imagine
Hepzibah, all those escaped lives
billowing in concerto

           now that it is freshly
sounding, now that you are
returned, more plausibly than
heroine

       to play it over and over

restitution

sleep's wakeful mode, its profusion hours
reckoning on one finger the lives of one
feather, where either fletcher or flight
to keep the breast warm, the small
hurrying days anxious to talk
only of unwinnable Iraq as
an end's intrusive mess, unnumbed also
to a suffering's violence, therefore how heads
cannot in safe purity expect to lay themselves
upon down pillows and hear *thank you*
or excessively to drown out, there and there
how the rich world in its pity, is buying up
children—in salvage the long wounded conflict

visa as pessimist

i

arrival may not be possible
what companionway

of safe passage
could you pick with confidence

from among
the jostling signs?

among the tossed lives
who reach the coastline

you are among the first
and last

who will be answered
with confusion

ii

in the country of few taps
succour can dry up like water

bones slip and sift
incomplete as archaeology

and present only as clues
—they might mourn

if it would achieve
but among spinifex

a passion for the succulent
goes untended

iii

the patter in the mouth
the patter in the feet

the great languages
of word and distance

—to lose where the life
was born and meet

a travelling caterpillar
on an outcrop of granite

its orange legs struggling
over dried fields of lichen

with less difficulty
than human arrival struggles

towards passport and place

iv

you could track
the caterpillar and learn

nothing more
than the desert hides

or between one timetable
and the next you could replace it

with an azure dragonfly
whose wings
                    (*O guard us
                    from our ecstacies*)

agitate the memories of flight
— in the ravaged lands

dread and shadelessness
move equally together

grief can make of travel
a family where faces   were

family *Roseacea*

having just discovered
this is the strawberry's
tree   of the roses
family of beautiful glow
and desirable smell
no way of knowing tho'

if they're imported
or locally grown
arriving by punnet
they're generic
less heart shaped
than they're described

it's becoming food-like
to arrive disguised
an artifice an additive
a future's genetics:
supply any delicacy
and make hunger submit

to eat this fruit therefore
would be to tongue-stroke
the bank roll
of any chief executive?
untouched it could be jam
for the next arrival

it could be the meal
for a long detention
from refugee to leaky
boat to barbed wire—
the fruit of travel
meets new starvation?

to proffer strawberry
as posy of welcome
to offer the tillage
of Eden in the eager
markets   it would
mean faking ownership

the fruit knife's
a more succinct edge
at least it's stainlessly overt
a steel alive at the throat
each slice into flesh a chant
each a blatant economy:

>*my quota*
>*my subsidy*
>*my sweet sweet red*

great-aunt narrative among the excised islands

'*oh my Canberra . . .*
high city of presumptive cleanness

among the dirty waters exuding
from the workplaces

the smell of your refusal laws
—throw gold dust and it would not glitter

with enough camouflage   gild, how
useful, its ticking riches, its shining tricks

as now it sets off the smoke, the alarms
the exclusion zones break through the

careful plaster and all the files are ASIOs—
too much pretty money is killing the sex slaves

the furore excavates silence, activism
is in the smoking heaps

everywhere the bartered workers die
it hurts the pocket to say these things

expect no free sex from the groundworks
erecting doors for the happy trade

the big island and the little islands
being moved further off only from

sexless asylum hands who do not titillate
knock knock, who's there?

from Capital Hill you can watch the navy
towing the latest boat away *chug chug*

it says *chug chug* as all its cargo
disbelieves and poorly fades'

census of the beloved

namyrna, out of your head comes such writings!
insepojeh namyrna, her real names
in disguise against deportation
'in England it is so far discovered'
that the names of a thousand infants
dead within their first year have been
stolen and given, the fibrillated 'illegals'
who now own them shift and shift
and still the postage stamps following them
like tattoos—*namyrna*, each day the gift of
anxious waking, each time you bathe, the soap
inflaming your infancy   quiver the fontanelles
this body your towel our conjoined fingerprints
how to breathe quietly, how not to falter when
touch burns   the questions, entries, exits
the hours given over to practice   how to live
nonchalantly in the twined life's furtive rooms

dis-locations…a polemic

'Do you think for a moment we were human beings to them?'
Carolyn Forché

1 *née* boat

'*when feet are refused land*
let them dance on the bloody waves

the opinion polls karaoke and constant
singing as from a bartered heaven

the feet asking for earth, air, fire, water
everything perilous and exposed, how do
they dream of us in their internal oceans?

on the nights fear flows through anxious blood
stellar money brings the spaceships home, all
our dangerous corridors where passions rend

asleep or not asleep on intravenous land
our cradle boat our shipwreck ownership
as all the votes held in our island hands'

2 navigation aid

'there's nothing that cannot be written
or be accused   an *us*, a *country*
a defence force's *enforcement of the law*
as in *Australia against* the Tampa rescuees

as also *against* the drowned ones of the
SIEV X , and the others, how many, how
lost   as if we practise gross remedies
to feed the sea's great slop   as if under

the bribe of a coast pulled tight:

> *thank you, yours sincerely*
> *do not join us on the shore'*

3   a manner of arrival

'to continue waking is to believe
anything is possible

for years a father . . .

> (not one of those detained
> on soil we'd call foreign to *him*
> but one still at home in the idea of being *safe*)
>
> . . . will tell of how

his daughter one morning
woke him with an arrival
that would burn him

how many steps it took
to reach the unknown vehicle

in his subsistence yard
he may not remember

but how can he forget the scar
he was given as a handshake

by one of the nervous men
occupying the car

who said he was only waiting
for a friend, and who then

moments later, drove off
and used himself

as a human bomb
so that the father

when he learned of it
understood he had shaken

hands with fire
and that his daughter also

was burnt
because she believed

in the act of awakening'

4   internment

'listen, the heart can suture itself
against rejection, but when love enters
the needle is a deeper ache

the point of you not you-as-delivery
from the ocean inside me but you
as perhaps-daughter who asks more
than birth and its infant languages

and all I've given you
is a vast interior of your own
a bag to breed your own life in
spirit of water, spirit of blood
little lung, alive in the breath,
breathing, breathed upon

your name in the old language generic
and rubric, a *little white Australian*
thumbprinted under Barton's 50-word
dictation test, words as lions and tigers
against *contamination by inferior races*

but now, and again now
2002/2003, summer:

> water under ration
> southern bushfires, northern ice storms
> at the high end of consumption
> the earth holding its breath
> against what we might next do
> hospitals full of the dead, the newborn
> *engineered, natural, perfect, flawed*
> and of the traumatised, rain and reign
> conflating, to encompass a deluge:
> *terrorism* and its huge new cup

the world in it, brim and elbow
viciousness and faith, and the drains
that sluice our rubbish into the seas
landing everything again and again
back into our mouths, back *home*
back *here*—the tourism
of an *economic necessity*

is it cowardice to want
to contaminate nothing?
I'd sew into your first pocket
a benison for the journey
whose boat both day and night
pyre and hope, leaky, historical
is heading always for land'

focal geology (1)

this the year I thought to have found it and have not
who would begin at the heart? who at the ear, the tongue?

ants come to forage and carry off nothing
it behaves like a river
sluicing off each leaf, each finger clinging

yesterday it dislodged a breast, today an eye
it drinks no milk and is blind
yet still it lies here listening

to voices of unbearable sentiment
singing of O home of the dream I lost

tomorrow more will come
trying to touch its eyes with their own
what can it say that it has not already said?

be at peace in your mouth
except that it has no voice, that it has lain

here infinitely to promote no proof
flowers keep appearing at the boundary
I named it once after one of the dead

this the year I thought to have found it and have not

focal geology (2)

instructions for engaging with a site:

which makes what sense on a pizza night's
dark prowl of cars slewed and stopped
by an escaped deer's graceful trot, tangle

of headlights, tango of engines, deer, hot
fuel, fuelled blood, strange antlers

how they are calm: picture *disdain*
high-held against the hungry monies
moaning in the pockets

—sweep of the wild eye (panic *could* be building)
the abated klaxons, something being paid for

how will you tell of this later? the cold night
trapped in a swirl vapour, breath,
exhausts, animal, drivers, cars, each

an introduced and the low mountain
years before cut through to make this crash

perhaps you will speak of tariffs
as the boundaries we pay
for having crossed—   does only

the tilted mind write rush poetry
as if whatever lives must utter itself swiftly
from where it stands on thixotropic clay

everywhere feet dying in mud
everywhere hands

in help or pushing them under,
the accident eyes, the shine of smashed glass
which inform us we are here, in heightened

air, our nebulae faces blue and orbital
in a condition of being planetary

the particular makers of an atmosphere

Other poetry titles from Spinifex Press

Wire Dancing

Patricia Sykes

Circus as drama and risk.

"In poems that are at once allusive and elusive, Sykes leaps
like an acrobat between past and present, mythology and
history, the everyday and the exotic, from Bosnia to the
circus. And dancing nimbly along the high wires of emotion
and intellect, she is passionate, witty, erudite and ironic . . .
I urge you . . . to buy and read this book so you can share
. . . what could be the poetry experience of the year."

— Bev Roberts

ISBN: 1-875559-90-6

The Wings of Angels

Sandy Jeffs

Not since Sylvia Plath and Anne Sexton has anyone written so candidly about madness. Able to manipulate key images, she moves from Niobe in "widow's shroud" to Kali in a regal gown of grotesque death. The way is memorably peopled by the Pilot, the Hand, the guardian of the Gate—a modern Cerberus with three heads: Ken, Barbie and Ronald McDonald.

ISBN: 1-876756-51-9

Poems from the Madhouse

Sandy Jeffs

"I read and read—and was profoundly moved. I delighted in it as poetry; I was touched by its honesty, courage and vulnerability."

— Anne Deveson

"Sandy Jeffs powerfully creates madness as cultural institution and social inscape . . . her argument is at once ravishingly intimate and brilliantly convincing."

— Kerry Leves, *Overland*

ISBN: 1-876756-03-9

Blood Relations

Sandy Jeffs

"Sandy Jeffs' poems inhabit the darkness at the heart of the dysfunctional family. The ravaged emotionality of these poems will speak to anyone who has felt its pain."

— Doris Brett

"A series of poems with a theatrical quality that is haunting in its exposure of the ritualistic violence perpetrated in the family home . . . These poems emerge like flowers on top of boiling water."

— Jeltje, *Five Bells*

ISBN: 1-875559-98-1

Feminist Fables

Suniti Namjoshi

An ingenious reworking of fairytales. Mythology mixed with the author's original material and vivid imagination. An indispensable feminist classic.

"Her imagination soars to breathtaking heights."

— Kerry Lyon, *Australian Book Review*

ISBN: 1-875559-19-1

St Suniti and the Dragon

Suniti Namjoshi

Ironic, fantastic, elegant and elegiac, fearful and funny. A thoroughly modern fable

"It's hilarious, witty, elegantly written, hugely inventive, fantastic, energetic."   — U. A. Fanthorpe

ISBN: 1-875559-18-3

The Body in Time / Nervous Arcs

Diane Fahey / Jordie Albiston

Two award-winning poets brought together in this finely wrought collection.

Diane Fahey's work has been described as having "integrity and incomparable delicacy" — Annie Greet, while Janette Turner Hospital writes of Jordie Albiston's collection that it has "sharp intelligence, lyrical grace and moral passion."

ISBN: 1-875559-37-X

Summer Was a Fast Train Without Terminals

Merlinda Bobis

An epic of the old Philippines, lyric reflections on longing, and an erotic dance drama make up this fine collection.

"Bobis can produce some genuinely haunting pieces. This is a touching work from an established poet."

— Hamesh Wyatt

ISBN: 1-875559-76-0

Bird

Susan Hawthorne

"Many-eyed and many-lived is this poet, as seismologist or lover, bird or newborn child. To the classic figures of Sappho or Eurydice she brings all the Now! Here! sense of discovery that fires her modern girl taking lessons in flight."

— Judith Rodriguez

ISBN: 1-875559-88-4

Charts and Soundings

Sue Fitchett and Jane Zusters

A luminous collection of photographs and poetry based in the New Zealand landscape. The poems angle the landscape, shimmer in the light of reflections on water, and sing cityscapes.

ISBN: 0-473-06192-9

Sybil: The Glide of Her Tongue

Gillian Hanscombe

A book where the lesbian voice mediates the essential vitality of she-dykes who have visions. A book where Gillian Hanscombe's poetry opens up meaning in such a way that it provides for beauty and awareness, for a space where one says yes to a lesbian we of awareness.

"Gillian Hanscombe is one of the most insightfully ironic, deliciously lyrical voices we have writing today."

— Betsy Warland

ISBN: 1-875559-05-1

*If you would like to know more about Spinifex Press,
write for a free catalogue or visit our website*

Spinifex Press
PO Box 212 North Melbourne
Victoria 3051 Australia